EARTH
BLESSINGS

Also by June Cotner

Amazing Graces
Animal Blessings
Baby Blessings
Back to Joy
Bedside Prayers
Bless the Beasts
Bless the Day
Christmas Blessings
Comfort Prayers
Dog Blessings
Family Celebrations
Forever in Love
Garden Blessings
Get Well Wishes
Graces
Gratitude Prayers
Heal Your Soul, Heal the World
The Home Design Handbook
House Blessings
Looking for God in All the Right Places
Miracles of Motherhood
Mothers and Daughters
Pocket Prayers
Say a Little Prayer: A Journal
Serenity Prayers
Soar! Follow Your Dreams
Teen Sunshine Reflections
To Have and To Hold
Toasts
We Are Women
Wedding Blessings
Wishing You Well

EARTH BLESSINGS

PRAYERS, POEMS AND MEDITATIONS

BY JUNE COTNER

VIVA
EDITIONS

Published in the United States by Viva Editions, an imprint of Start Midnight,
LLC, 101 Hudson Street, 37th Floor, Suite 3705, Jersey City, NJ 07302

Printed in the United States.
Cover design: Scott Idleman/Blink
Cover photograph: iStock
Text design: Frank Wiedemann

First Edition.
10 9 8 7 6 5 4 3 2 1

Trade paper ISBN: 978-1-63228-023-7
E-book ISBN: 978-1-63228-027-5

DEDICATION

For Brenda Knight—
Thanks so much for believing in the importance
of publishing *Earth Blessings.*

For the staff of Viva Editions—
I'm deeply grateful for your work in support of this book.

"There are no passengers on spaceship earth. We are all crew."
—MARSHALL MCLUHAN

Contents

Letter to Readers

As a child I was always drawn to the outdoors…as an adult, I still am! Some of the most memorable times in my life have been spent surrounded by nature. To this day, I continue to hike regularly—and I honestly don't know where I would be without the solace of wilderness.

But we don't need to be in the wilderness to experience the beauty of nature. At home, I continue to be astonished by the everyday marvels that surround me—birds, plants, animals, sky, sunshine, and moonlight. These things serve as reminders that we can carry nature with us wherever we go.

It was the book *Silent Spring* by Rachel Carson that first drew my attention to the fragile nature of the environment. I read it in college and her words opened my mind to the notion that human actions could affect the very ecosystems upon which our lives depend.

Where would we be if we did not have Mother Earth to rely upon?

How can we view humanity, if not through the lens that is the world around us? And what does the state of the world today say to our communities and to our children?

It is my belief that the sacred can be found not in things abstract and ethereal, but in the earth itself. I hope that, by reading this anthology, we may all come to realize what a vital place the earth holds, not only in our relationships with one another, but in our relationships with the world we live in.

Many books have been written on the practical aspects of living green, but only a few focus on the spiritual. I set out to create a book that would be an ecological celebration, complete with inspiring poems, interfaith prayers, and spiritual prose. In *Earth Blessings,* I have chosen selections from over ten years' worth of collected material, pieces that authentically speak to the earth and to the intricate ties that bind us to it.

I have been compiling anthologies for twenty years and my contributors now number over nine hundred. The inclusion of contemporary writers, such as Kelly Cherry, Barbara Crooker, Michael S. Glaser, and Ellen Bass, provides a freshness and originality that is not found in other collections. In addition, I have included wisdom from environmental advocates such as Rachel Carson, Al Gore, Tom Hayden, Bill McKibben, and John Muir (among others); as well as classic pieces by well-known authors such as John Burroughs, John Keats, Rainer Maria Rilke, and Walt Whitman.

As Henry David Thoreau said, "Live your beliefs and you can turn the world around." I hope this book will encourage us to look more deeply at our unique planet with a global awareness and respect, to gently remind us to do our part in sustaining an environmentally friendly lifestyle, and to cherish Earth for the presence of the divine that appears to us through the natural world.

June Cotner
P.O. Box 2765
Poulsbo, WA 98370
www.junecotner.com

Thanks

I was thrilled to find my publisher, Brenda Knight, who shared my vision for this book and was so excited to acquire it! My profound gratitude is reflected in my dedication page to Brenda and her excellent staff at Viva Editions.

This book would have not become a reality without the support of my two excellent literary agents, Denise Marcil and Anne Marie O'Farrell, at Marcil-O'Farrell Literary. Denise, thanks for believing in this book for more than a decade. Anne Marie, thank you for your for help in bringing this book to Viva Editions. I continue to be inspired and energized by both of you. As agents and as friends, I deeply appreciate your honest feedback and insightful suggestions that make my anthologies stronger. It's so much fun to brainstorm with both of you!

For the contributors to *Earth Blessings*, I have worked with some of you for twenty years when your poems and prayers were included in my first two collections, *Graces* and *Bedside Prayers* (both published by HarperOne). Kelly Cherry, Barbara Crooker, Corrine De Winter, Susan J. Erickson, Theresa Mary Grass, Maryanne Hannan, C. David Hay, Shirley Kobar, Arlene Gay Levine, Gary E. McCormick, Hilda Lachney Sanderson, and Joanna M. Weston—we go back for two decades! I'm always so thrilled to find a publisher who can showcase your fine work.

For the staff at Viva Editions, I appreciate how hard you work to design such beautiful books. Your devotion to the mission of creating "books for vivacious living" is reflected by the considerable time you take to make these books successful. I'm glad to be on your team!

My heartfelt gratitude goes to my husband, Jim Graves, and my many relatives and friends who encourage and inspire me every day.

And lastly, I'm grateful to God who has given me a career I love and has put me in touch with so many wonderful contributors and resources which enable me to bring inspirational collections into the world.

NATURE AND THE ENVIRONMENT

Look at Nature's beauty and perfection—
everything is so joyful!

—AMMA

NATURE SPEAKS TO ME

The beauty of the trees,
the softness of the air,
the fragrance of the grass,
speaks to me.

The summit of the mountain,
the thunder of the sky,
the rhythm of the sea,
speaks to me.

The faintness of the stars,
the freshness of the morning,
the dewdrop of the flower,
speaks to me.

The strength of the fire,
the taste of salmon,
the trail of the sun,
and the life that never goes away,
they speak to me.

And my heart soars.

—CHIEF DAN GEORGE

IT IS GOOD

We are rooted to the air through our lungs and to the soil through our stomachs. We are walking trees and floating plants. The soil which in one form we spurn with our feet, and in another take into our mouths and into our blood—what a composite product it is!... The soil underfoot, or that we turn with our plow, how it thrills with life or the potencies of life! What a fresh, good odor it exhales when we turn it with our spade or plow in spring! It is good.

—JOHN BURROUGHS

THE HOH RIVER AND RAINFOREST:
A HAIKU SEQUENCE

colonnade of trees—
reminder of the nurse log
that once sustained them

Western red cedar—
coastal people called it
"the long life-maker"

rushing glacier stream
tumbled rough river stones smooth—
we palm them with joy

deer wade glacier stream
maple flames on the far bank
autumn approaches

vast wings crack the sky
above gray snag's jagged crown—
ospreys feeding young

sun-dappled glade
female elk browses the tips
of saw-toothed sword fern

—SUZANNE C. COLE

SPIRIT EAR

After a line by Rumi

Let your spirit ear listen
to the green dome's passionate murmur.
Ferns burst from the earth,
their coiled heads muted cymbals
in spring's orchestra.
From the topmost branch of a cedar
a Bewick's wren sways and trills
about something that translates as happiness
in a language with neither noun nor verb.
Water and wind, chords of clouds,
a crescendo of light.

—SUSAN J. ERICKSON

FIG GROVE

I know how to find it now,
but for years, I would stumble
into the grove, unprepared
for its enchantments, the coolness
of its air, the dapple of its light,
the way the large fig trees
stand with their arms wide open.

They are the sexiest trees I've ever
seen, if trees can be sexy, the most
muscular, if trees can be muscular,
their silvery skin sinuous and tendony,
dancers holding space between leaps.
They bring me right back into my own
skin, invite me to press myself against
their cool, smooth, bark, to climb into
their limbs and rest myself in any
number of their crotches. *Welcome,*
welcome, they say, *welcome home.*
And then there's the one tree
that fruits all over its body,
figs springing even from the trunk,
every part of it bursting

into seed, as if it can't contain
itself, as if every cell wants to break
into song, and that's how I feel
when I stand in its presence, taking in
its sugary breath—each part of me
alive, explosive, down to
the deepest, plainest root.

—GAYLE BRANDEIS

THE PLACE NO ONE KNEW

I went there for solitude and restoration.
It was a place at the edge of a silver lake,
where I could go and smell the forest.

No one knew about my secret altar,
except for some chipmunks and a blue heron.

Yet concealed under a canopy of birch leaves,
my love began:

for rocks
for trees
for water
for God.

—MIKE W. BLOTTENBERGER

UNTO THE HILLS

Before drifting into the cerulean yonder,
inhale the healing breath of mountain brooks,
alpine bluebells, and lodgepole pine.
Exhale—a warm, cactus-flower desert wind,
a tincture of ambrosial vine and elderberry wine

Listen to wishes-on-wings flutter down misty canyons;
echoes of angels wings, instant messengers
rising and dissolving into the starry incandescence,
the timeless celestial symphony

Then, like snowflakes, floating, rocking, slip-sliding back down
the high country rainbow—inhale

—BOB MCCRAY

THE INN IN THE CEDARS

Come, walk with me,
And see the distant breasts of trees—
Glimmering notes beneath the sky
Anointing the thoughts of passer-by.

Come, stand awhile,
And watch the sun wash the brush,
And brown brittle stalks of circling rush.

Come delight with me,
And listen to the breeze
Sweeping the leaves—

Listen for its soft whisper
Binding the mind
To the cadence of life,
The song of love,
And beauty's breadth.

—ANNIE DOUGHERTY

SEPTEMBER'S EARLY DUSK

(A Ghazal)

In the thin light of the waking crescent moon, yellow
becomes brown. Pinecones turn to silver at our feet.

Raptors now sleep in trees on the mountain. Splayed
pine needles wave a warm welcome to the cooling wind.

Mountains themselves are darker than the night sky. The
crickets sing, and we listen through the song to hear the notes.

These clouds have arrived like silk curtains on a window.
Although we cannot see, we know the stars are up there, dancing.

—CATHY CAPOZZOLI

THE NATURAL WORLD

I believe a leaf of grass is no less than the journey-work of the stars.

—WALT WHITMAN

I go to nature to be soothed and healed, and to have my senses put in order.

—JOHN BURROUGHS

Earth and sky, woods and fields, lakes and rivers, the mountain and the sea, are excellent schoolmasters, and teach some of us more than we can ever learn from books.

—JOHN LUBBOCK

Climb the mountains and get their good tidings. Nature's peace will flow into you as the sunshine into the trees. The winds will blow their freshness into you, and the storms their energy, while cares will drop off like autumn leaves.

—JOHN MUIR

I think the environment should be put in the category of our national security. Defense of our resources is just as important as defense abroad. Otherwise what is there to defend?

—ROBERT REDFORD

I can't imagine anything more important than air, water, soil, energy and biodiversity. These are the things that keep us alive.

—DAVID SUZUKI

Our minds, as well as our bodies, have need of the out-of-doors. Our spirits, too, need simple things, elemental things, the sun and the wind and the rain, moonlight and starlight, sunrise and mist and mossy forest trails, the perfumes of dawn and the smell of fresh-turned earth and the ancient music of wind among the trees.

—EDWIN WAY TEALE

Come forth into the light of things, let nature be your teacher.

—WILLIAM WORDSWORTH

OCTOBER DUSK

The last of the light
ignites a yellow flame of poplar
and red sumac burns
against the approaching

dark, that spreads a muted wash
across the paler page of day.
The sky swallows
this white host of land,

slap-water sound of a beaver's tail
a benediction for the ungainly
pelicans, white robed penitents,
lingering on the riverbank.

Night is announced
by the cantor call of geese
sharp with yearning. Soon

the winds will rise, strip
the yellow fans from ginkgos, tremble
the last, last leaves from the sycamore
limbs, stately and bared, nothing,
nothing is left but the wanting.

—MAUREEN MCQUERRY

DUSK AT THE FARM

Fields lie beyond the green ditchwater,
clouds so dark they thin slowly. Here,
I wait for the light to grow dim, to churn
and bring the wind from the woods,
full of dormant children waiting to grow,
their tired eyes kissing the spring, sipping
water filled with the light of cherry blossoms,
with dusk's odors falling down
from the tree tops, the cedar spines,
and the large, aching maple that makes
me want to stop and rest, to breathe
and be joyful about the moonlight
and your eyes that are still and newborn
when they look at me, toward the clouds.

—LEONARD J. CIRINO

BLACKBERRY MAN

You rise at dawn, walk
the curving road to where
blackberries tumble on cluttered vines
grown wild and strong through summers'
heavy reach. Down the slope,
across the gully once musical
with rain, and there you are:
bucket hanging on sun-browned arm
and hands already picking.
Do you think *jewels*? Do you
imagine a hundred peacock eyes
in this wealth of glistening purple?
Enough to feel the tug and weight
of *berry*, food for eye and tongue,
the sun making its own slow color
across a sky where heat begins
to show you earth's true name.

—KATHARYN HOWD MACHAN

two

HONORING
THE EARTH

The Earth is alive and has a Soul.

—PAULO COELHO

THE EARTH'S DANCE

Let the trees stretch their arms
as the leaves frolic in tune
to the wind's waltz.

Let the mountains leap.

Let the oceans whirl their bodies
as the fish shimmy
to the current's refrain.

Let the rivers swing.

Let the rain tap a melody
as the animals prance
together in harmony.

Let the birds flap a song
to the beat of the breeze.

Let the earth continue to dance.

—ANNETTE GULATI

FAITH IN THE WATER

I see a stream with slow moving sections and patches of turbulence. I can sense it is drawn towards something bigger than itself—the lake sitting miles from its origin. I notice the water doesn't question where it's going—it just keeps moving.

I look at the rocks under the strong current and observe that they are still and solid. They remain secure enough not to lose their grounded and nurturing attachment to the earth while being incessantly thrust upon. I suspect they trust in their purpose to slow down the speed of the water.

Occasionally, I watch a leaf fall from its source. It lands in the stream and begins its way to the chaotic water. I ask myself if the leaf was clumsy and lost its true nature or if it was forced there by the winds because it was too stubborn to let go. No matter. It doesn't fight the inevitable or swim like mad to return where it came from. The leaf surrenders to the short lived patterns of being spun around, dunked, and flipped over, knowing she will make her way to a new stretch of calm water.

I take a deep breath by this stream and tell myself that it's time for more faith when my waters are turbulent, for more trust, and a stronger sense that I am moving where I need to go—a place I can't see yet, but know is there.

—CAROL COOLEY

MY MOTHER

The Earth is my Mother.
The wind is my Mother's breath.
Trees, flowers, birds and animals—
all are my beloved Mother.

The waves are my Mother's cheeks,
the stones my Mother's feet.
Trees, flowers, birds and animals—
all are my beloved Mother.

The stars are my Mother's crown.
The sun and moon are her eyes.
Trees, flowers, birds and animals—
all are my beloved Mother.

—JANINE CANAN

IN BEAUTY MAY I WALK

In beauty   may I walk
All day long   may I walk
Through the returning seasons   may I walk
Beautifully will I possess again
Beautifully birds
Beautifully joyful birds
On the trail marked with pollen   may I walk
With grasshoppers about my feet   may I walk
With dew about my feet   may I walk
With beauty   may I walk
With beauty before me   may I walk
With beauty behind me   may I walk
With beauty all around me   may I walk
In old age, wandering on a trail
          of beauty, lively,   may I walk
In old age, wandering on a trail
          of beauty, lively again,   may I walk
It is finished in beauty
It is finished in beauty

—AUTHOR UNKNOWN

NATURE NEAR HOME

(Excerpt from *Field and Study*)

After long experiences I am convinced that the best place to study nature is at one's own home—on the farm, in the mountains, on the plains, by the sea—no matter where that may be. One has it all about him then. The seasons bring to his door the great revolving cycle of wild life, floral and faunal, and he needs miss no part of the show.... Familiarity with things about one should not dull the edge of curiosity or interest. The walk you take today through the fields and woods, or along the riverbank, is the walk you should take tomorrow, and next day, and next. What you miss once, you will hit upon next time. The happenings are at intervals and are irregular. The play of Nature has no fixed program.

—JOHN BURROUGHS

THEOLOGY

Perhaps it is
enough to know
that a yellow sun

dripping

through a blue sky
can paint the forests
the deepest green.

—KENNETH SALZMANN

WHAT STRUCK ME MOST WAS THE SILENCE

What struck me most was the silence. It was a great silence, unlike any I have encountered on Earth, so vast and deep that I began to hear my own body: my heart beating, my blood vessels pulsing, even the rustle of my muscles moving over each other seemed audible. There were more stars in the sky than I had expected. The sky was deep black, yet at the same time bright with sunlight. The Earth was small, light blue, and so touchingly alone, our home that must be defended like a holy relic. The Earth was absolutely round. I believe I never knew what the word "round" meant until I saw Earth from space.

—ALEKSEI LEONOV
(Russian cosmonaut who took the first-ever spacewalk on March 18, 1965)

A PROVERB

To care
for Mother Earth
is to honor
her Maker.
To conserve
her precious gifts
is to honor
generations
yet
to
come.

—JOAN MARIE ARBOGAST

EARTH SPEAKS

Earth Speaks:
I am here.
I have always been
and always will be.
Walk into my arms,
Feel my breath,
Love me
As you would a friend.

—CORRINE DE WINTER

CUSTODIANS OF THE FUTURE

Only in the last quarter of my life have we come to know what it means to be custodians of the future of the Earth—to know that unless we care, unless we check the rapacious exploitations of our Earth and protect it, we are endangering the future of our children and our children's children. We did not know this before, except in little pieces. People knew that they had to take care of their own...but it was not until we saw the picture of the earth, from the moon, that we realized how small and how helpless this planet is—something that we must hold in our arms and care for.

—MARGARET MEAD

RESTORATION

I breathe,
Slowly through my nostrils
Capturing particles
Of air
That travel to my lungs, in harmony
With Life
Surrounding me.

I release an essence
With every parting breath,
Trees, flowers, weeds
Synthesize the gas
And exhale the oxygen
Through structures
As delicate as butterfly wings.
In our interdependence
We sanctify each other with Life
Each breath a blessing
A restoration, an act of healing.

—SHIRLEY KOBAR

TO CARE FOR THE EARTH

This Earth embodies the graceful act of creation,
life springing from Life, full and vibrant.
Within the unfolding story
of ancient drama and future world,
lies the wisdom of the ages.
Stand quietly on sacred ground;
listen to the heartbeat of the Earth.
We are one with this world,
with the life that flows within and around it,
streaming outward to the larger Life
that gave this planet its place
in our history and in our hearts.
To care for the Earth is to honor our souls.

—KAREN MINNICH-SADLER

three
CYCLES OF LIFE

You could not step twice into the same river;
for other waters are ever flowing on to you.

—HERACLITUS

WHEN YOU RETURN

Fallen leaves will climb back into trees.
Shards of the shattered vase will rise
and reassemble on the table.
Plastic raincoats will refold
into their flat envelopes. The egg,
bald yolk and its transparent halo,
slide back in the thin, calcium shell.
Curses will pour back into mouths,
letters unwrite themselves, words
siphoned up into the pen. My gray hair
will darken and become the feathers
of a black swan. Bullets will snap
back into their chambers, the powder
tamped tight in brass casings. Borders
will disappear from maps. Rust
revert to oxygen and time. The fire
return to the log, the log to the tree,
the white root curled up
in the unsplit seed. Birdsong will fly
into the lark's lungs, answers
become questions again.
When you return, sweaters will unravel
and wool grow on the sheep.

Rock will go home to mountain, gold
to vein. Wine crushed into the grape,
oil pressed into the olive. Silk reeled in
to the spider's belly. Night moths
tucked close into cocoons, ink drained
from the indigo tattoo. Diamonds
will be returned to coal, coal
to rotting ferns, rain to clouds, light
to stars sucked back and back
into one timeless point, the way it was
before the world was born,
that fresh, that whole, nothing
broken, nothing torn apart.

—ELLEN BASS

LULLABY FOR ONE AM

Tonight, I'm wedded to the moon.
Tomorrow it will be the dawn.
By noon the sun will dim.
At dusk my day will end.
As in dream, the world seems.

With the seasons, the hours pass,
each one fresh. Who'd ever guess
the face of earth could bless
our every act? We should ask,
what comes first, who comes last?

Spirit of the ghost, can I say,
I go from black and white to gray?
The darkness brings me gentle light,
I'm wedded to the moon, tonight.

—LEONARD J. CIRINO

GIVING BACK

All through the summers you took blue
of snowmelt lakes at timberline
and left them just as blue; took scent
of sage along the eastern slopes,
the lilt of mariposa lily on a granite
ridge. You took the ache of climbing
in your lungs, you tasted trail dust.

And so it's right that now we scatter
you like dust beside the trail; give you
to the leeward edge of juniper and pine,
to lupine and the larkspur's purple shade;
give you to the underside of snow
when it comes; to mud and stars. We spread
you like a breath of mist on meadow.

—TAYLOR GRAHAM

HEARTWOOD: A DIARY

> Stouter ones hold heartwood at the center.
> *—THE OBSERVER'S BOOK OF TREES*

The secret lies in the winter-resting buds
and *cambium*, a tissue one cell thick.
Or, what makes trees tick?

Consider conifers,
the broad-leaved beech and ash,
the oak on Auclum Close,
how light rests on their branches
like birds' nests—out of reach,
full of flight.

November 1ˢᵗ.
Night. Write:
Lichen lives on a knob of bark.
A tree is a growing stick.
These truths are a way to knowing dark.

February. It's snowing.
All day I sit at my desk.
At four o'clock the snow stops,

the wind stops, the world stops,
and I go out to gaze on my shadow,
cool as meltwater.

The weeks unwind, like a ribbon unfurled.

Spring moves north
at the rate of sixteen miles a day,
a green clay.
Shape into leaves, grass;
fire and glaze.
These are the *ways* of the world:
to dig and plant, bake in the sun.

All things come to fruition.

—KELLY CHERRY

CYCLES

A lake in all its different moods
waits the way we wait
for grace. Even a lake
loves the sprinkle
of new rain on its face,
as if it has forgotten
what it's made of. It's all grace—
as the marriage of earth and sky
is an intricate rhythm
of call and response,
the sky recycling itself
so it can give to the earth again,
water rising only to return.

Water, like God, comes to us
in three forms, makes frequent
surprise appearances,
and goes by many different names,
yet its essence is the same
on earth as it is in heaven.
Water remembers every need.
It speaks every language.

—EMILY RUTH HAZEL

AFTER THE LONG GATHERING

After the long gathering
You will enter a silence
Of stones,
Of leaves,
Of wings.

You will hear
That when anything ends
A singing begins.

This singing has been
Part of you
Since the beginning of time.
It comes to break the tide,
To pierce the dark
And make you green again.

After the long gathering
You will enter a silence
Of stones,
Of leaves,
Of wings.

—CORRINE DE WINTER

A FIELD IN AUGUST

In the last fine days of August
we find the field of Queen Anne's Lace,
a confusion of snowflakes nodding
on their woody stems to the music
of cicadas.

The dog buries his nose in tall grasses,
chuffing in a world of scents beyond
my ken while I take the sunlight
into my skin, and the cool breeze
that's just now skimmed toward us
from the lake.

This is the dog that came to us
on the eve of a blizzard, skinny
and scarred, shivering hard—
yelping on our doorstep.

This is the field that months ago
was weighted with snow, drifts
that wouldn't let go. The flowers
teetering up toward summer's clear
dry light seem to remember

something of that. You'll say this
can't be true; a thatch of flowering
weed has no capacity for imagination.
The dog leans into my leg, looking
up at me. A fly lands on his back
and he shivers it off.

I say each season, each body, each
living field holds some memory
of days past, some whiff of days to come.

—GINNY LOWE CONNORS

WHAT THE RIVER SAID

I ran to the river in spring
and the river laughed, "Flow."
I ambled to the river in summer
and the river urged, "Grow."
I walked to the river in autumn
and the river cried, "See!"
I arrived at the river in winter
and the river whispered, "Be."

—ARLENE GAY LEVINE

SEASON OF SURPRISES

Since early memory, I've eagerly awaited the arrival of spring, like a child waits for Christmas morning. Sweet lilacs, Easter lilies all dressed up in white satin, rose buds poking out noses to test the air—all delight my senses and my heart.

Flowers graced the makeshift altars of my childhood. I preferred flowers more my size—buttercups, violets, dandelions. They grew closer to the ground I laid on, played on, dreamed upon—where I always searched for surprises: a new variety, a different color, four-leaf clovers.

I treasure them still, those tiny blooms, those perky little heads that pop up everywhere across meadows and hillsides, but now I leave them to be discovered and gathered by younger dreamers.

The flower gardens planted by my grandmother and the vegetable gardens sown each year by my family were spectacular, plentiful and delicious because our hands had watered and cared for them. But it's the abundance of flowers in deserts, on mountains, in the meadows of the world, tended by unseen hands, that continues to renew my faith in a generous and loving Creator. And I've learned that spring is eternal if we continue to seek the surprises.

—MARY LENORE QUIGLEY

REMEMBER

Remember the bread that you eat,
The fields where the grains grew,
The sun that made it live,
The water that fed it,
The hands that created bread from it.
Be mindful.
Remember everything and everyone
That loved you into being.
Remember why you are here,
Who sang to you when you feared,
Who waited for you
When you felt like you were getting nowhere.
Remember that all life matters
And give thanks for it.

—CORRINE DE WINTER

EACH IN ITS OWN TIME

Live in each season as it passes; breathe the air, drink the drink, taste the fruit.

—HENRY DAVID THOREAU

Our goal is not to get out of the world or to get out of life, but to integrate it, to celebrate it, to embrace it fully, and to embrace all the different cycles within it.

—STARHAWK

Every living thing of the ocean, plant and animal alike, returns to the water at the end of its own life span the materials which had been temporarily assembled to form its body. Thus, individual elements are lost to view, only to reappear again and again in different incarnation in a kind of material immortality.

—RACHEL CARSON

Nature does not hurry, yet everything is accomplished.

—LAO TZU

four

LIVING SIMPLY

Live simply that others may simply live.

—MAHATMA GANDHI

A CONCEPT OF GRACE

Consider the green
in your garden—
The peas and lettuce,
the peppers and broccoli,
the tomatoes, onions
carrots and potatoes

how sweetly your body
celebrates each tasty morsel:
no artificial colors, or flavors
chemicals or hormones,
no warnings, not even labels

just seeds to soil
to blossom to fruit
to your table.

—MICHAEL S. GLASER

HAPPINESS

I asked the professors who teach the meaning of life to tell
me what is happiness.

And I went to famous executives who boss the work of
thousands of men.

They all shook their heads and gave me a smile as though
I was trying to fool with them

And then one Sunday afternoon I wandered out along
the Desplaines river

And I saw a crowd of Hungarians under the trees with
their women and children and a keg of beer and an
accordion.

—CARL SANDBURG

BLESSED WITH SIMPLICITY

Be content with what you have;
rejoice in the way things are.
When you realize there is nothing lacking,
the whole world belongs to you.

—LAO TZU

I went to the woods because I wished to live deliberately, to front only
the essential facts of life, and see if I could not learn what it had to
teach, and not, when I came to die, discover that I had not lived.

—HENRY DAVID THOREAU

The day, water, sun, moon, night—
I do not have to purchase these things with money.

—PLAUTUS

Maybe a person's time would be as well spent
raising food as raising money to buy food.

—FRANK A. CLARK

I learned to live simply, and I learned to get a great joy out of work…. I
grew up to believe wholly and completely in men and women who live
simply, frugally and in fine faith.

—GEORGE NORRIS

To find the universal elements enough; to find the air and the water
exhilarating; to be refreshed by a morning walk or an evening
saunter…to be thrilled by the stars at night; to be elated over a bird's
nest or a wildflower in spring—these are some of the rewards of the
simple life.

—JOHN BURROUGHS

Precisely the least, the softest, lightest, a lizard's rustling, a breath, a
flash, a moment—a little makes the way of the best happiness.

—FRIEDRICH NIETZSCHE

CODA

The wind pulls a drawstring of clouds
around the sun, tucks that jewel
into the vest pocket of the horizon.

Shadows touch across the grass
as children toast the coming dark
with laughter.

The day completes itself in bird song.

—MARTHA CHRISTINA

SIMPLICITY

The forgotten skirt in prairie print
hangs limply from the peg in the cabin
where we come to live without the
finery we crave.

Here the weeds are flowers, the birds our
sirens and the brook our music. Here we
lie in bed piled with quilts. The light goes fast
and the fire dies down with the sighing
of the woods.

Talking in hushed tones not to compete with the stars,
we slow to the rhythms of our breathing. Asleep
in the cradle of God.

—JANICE A. FARRINGER

GIFTS TO YOURSELF

Rise with the sun
Stretch with the breeze
Serve food with prayers
Nap after the noon
Sleep with the moon

—SALLY CLARK

THE BEST SEASON

Ten thousand flowers in spring,
the moon in autumn,
a cool breeze in summer,
snow in winter.
If your mind isn't clouded by
unnecessary things,
this is the best season of your life.

—WU-MEN

five

OUR CHILDREN

Earth's beauty—
as mighty as your tiny hand in mine.

—NANCY TUPPER LING

GOLDEN PEARL

Let it be true
that people are a blessed
and desired thing.
That we would walk lightly
upon the world's cheek,
like butterfly kisses,
a mother's eyelashes
tenderly flirting.
Hummingbirds and
Halleluiah choirs.
Blue Herons as they
turn and face the dawn.
Let our children come
to sing the praise of the cosmos,
to declare their journey glorious.
Let them not forget
the light and sound,
the tunnel of song
through which they were born.
Look how Day returns
from Midnight's traveling dream,
opening tenderly its palm
to release the bird that is the sun,
a golden pearl, an offering.

—INGRID GOFF-MAIDOFF

FIRST GRANDCHILD

I pat your back,
coaxing the bubbles up,
that happy milk-drunk look upon your face.
Your little back, my little drum,
I sing "Imagine."
I couldn't have imagined
when this song was new
that we'd be handing you the world
still unrepaired.

I want to take you to the woods.
I want the trees to be your teachers.
The white pine and the maples
and the mountain ash, growing up
out of the same patch of earth
shoulder to shoulder, roots entwined.

All over the world, your sisters and brothers
are springing up…first breath, first light,
first arms to hold them.
You burp, bobble your head
and fall asleep.
Your life is right here
in my hands.

—DEBORAH GORDON COOPER

WHAT I WANT TO TELL YOU ABOUT THE RAIN

for my niece

1. There will be seasons of longing
as the earth, your mouth, your mind
cry out for water. Faith, in this time,
will shimmer as it beckons and disappears.

2. Suddenly it will come. Your tongue,
out the car window, will greet it.
You will gulp it, be greedy.
You forget all your fears.

3. And then you grow weary,
miss the bees and the birds
and the wide wave of sunlight.
All is puddles and tears.

4. This is the thing about rain
that I want to tell you:
It will come. It will go.
The sooner you learn this,
the better. I should know.

—CASSIE PREMO STEELE

LITTLE EYES

Oh, to see the world again
Through the eyes of a tiny child;
To marvel at the mysteries
Of all things tamed and wild.

The blossom of a flower,
Bright diamonds in the snow,
To watch the flight of birds
And dream of where they go.

The dance of dainty butterflies,
Trees that touch the sky,
Enchantment of all creatures
That run or swim or fly.

Countless thrills are awaiting
The touch of a tiny hand;
Adventure's just a step away
In the place called Wonderland.

Every road is one not taken,
Each day brings a new surprise.
God must have made this all—
Just for little eyes.

—C. DAVID HAY

FOR THE CHILDREN

They will eat the fruits of our labors
If we labor enough to bear fruit
For if not now, when?
Let us see their hopeful faces
Smiling at a healthy world
And let that be all the nourishment we need.

—CHERYL PAULSON

Oh great planet of our birth, the mother of life,
may we learn your wisdom so that our children's children
will revel in your wealth.

—NITA PENFOLD

GO AHEAD

Imagine a baby, mother and father.
Have them sit together on a bench
in dappled sunlight, or lie, playing
on a blanket. Let them hear birdsong.
Let them breathe loamy earth,
the wafting scent of pine.
The day is coming to an end.

Don't discard the sentimental
image. It won't hurt you.
It may even cast its lightness
on you. Befriend beauty
and innocence and simplicity.
We owe it to ourselves;
we owe it to that baby.

—MARYANNE HANNAN

COPPER, GOLD, RUSSET

Along the narrow trail
children rushing ahead
we hear the forest's cascade
– falling, falling, layers
protecting tender seedlings.

We point out spruce, madrone
offer glints of knowledge
like golden flakes drifting
landing in their soft hair.

—ARLENE L. MANDELL

SUMMER EVENING INTERLUDE

When late-day shadows lengthen
    and a long day tends toward night,
Our children settle down from play,
    and the house grows calm and quiet.
The weariness of working is
    forgotten while we share
The good and bad that's been our day,
    from a favorite easy chair.
A cool wind finds a window
    opened just to let it in.
The lightning bugs and crickets
    seemed everywhere again.
With dishes done and drying, and
    all problems put on hold,
A shaft of fading sunlight
    lights up our room with gold.
The gold falls on our children.
    You reach to hold my hand.
My fingers curl to fit in yours.
    You touch my wedding band.
It's then that family ties grow strong,
    and caring tightly binds,
And leaves, and weaves fond memories
    in the crannies of our minds.

—ALICE T. WEGER

SUMMER SOLSTICE

Come, bring the children. Let them
feel for a moment the rhythm
of the hoe. Let them experience
the wonder of green shoots emerging
from earth, earth given us
in guardianship from the Creation.

Body, mind, and spirit full to bursting
with ripe, sweet berries, the first
tender green beans, and corn. We give
thanks, and thanks again. The twin
concepts of Reason and Peace are
seen in each kernel of an ear of corn.

Perhaps we repair our lodges
as do the beavers living close by.
Our children swim like river otters
and as their laughter reaches us,
we join them for a while
in these hottest of summer days.

—PETER BLUE CLOUD

six

HONORING ANIMALS

Listening to the birds can be a meditation
if you listen with awareness.

—OSHO

ON THE GRASSHOPPER AND CRICKET

The poetry of earth is never dead:
    When all the birds are faint with the hot sun,
    And hide in cooling trees, a voice will run
From hedge to hedge about the new-mown mead;
That is the Grasshopper's—he takes the lead
    In summer luxury,—he has never done
    With his delights; for when tired out with fun
He rests at ease beneath some pleasant weed.
The poetry of earth is ceasing never:
    On a lone winter evening, when the frost
      Has wrought a silence, from the stove there shrills
The Cricket's song, in warmth increasing ever,
    And seems to one in drowsiness half lost,
      The Grasshopper's among some grassy hills.

—JOHN KEATS

BLESS THE ANIMALS

Bless the animals of every form and size, wherever they may be. In a heartland or a coastline, in the pasture or the jungle, all are of God's creation.

Whether legged, winged, scaled, or finned, all creatures are precious to the circle of life. As they go about doing what is theirs to do, they make a positive difference in our world.

A tiny, wet-nosed puppy snuggles on a bed. The powerful burst of a whale's blow reaches for the sky. All animals give us reason to appreciate them.

They are handsome, strong, and giving. They give comfort, joy, safety, and service. It is our joy to take care of and protect them and their habitats. Wherever they may be, they are gifts of God, essential to the balance of nature.

—AUTHOR UNKNOWN

HOW BEAUTIFUL AND PERFECT ARE THE ANIMALS!

(Excerpt from *Leaves of Grass*)

How beautiful and perfect are the animals! How perfect is my soul!
How perfect the Earth, and the minutest thing on it!
What is called good is perfect, and what is called bad is just as perfect;
The vegetables and minerals are all perfect, and the imponderable
    fluids are perfect;
Slowly and surely they have passed on to this, and slowly and surely
    they yet pass on....
I swear I think there is nothing but immortality!

—WALT WHITMAN

STUDY THE WINTER BIRDS

(Excerpt from *Field and Study*)

If you would study the winter birds…you need not go to the winter woods to do so; you can bring them to your own door. A piece of suet on a tree in front of your window will bring chickadees, nuthatches, downy woodpeckers, brown creepers, and often juncos. And what interest you will take in these little waifs from the winter woods that daily or hourly seek the bounty you prepare for them! It is not till they have visited you for weeks that you begin to appreciate the bit of warmth and life they have added to your winter outlook. The old tree trunk then wears a more friendly aspect. The great inhospitable out-of-doors is relenting a little; the cold and the snow have found their match, and it warms your heart to think that you can help these brave little feathered people to win the fight.

—JOHN BURROUGHS

WILDLIFE

If we can teach people about wildlife, they will be touched. Share my wildlife with me. Because humans want to save things that they love.

—STEVE IRWIN

ALSO, THERE ARE THE KINDNESSES OF BIRDS

All kindness should be so disinterested. They never lie. Never proclaim that all is well. Never claim to bestow the truth. But they have such faith. Announcing each day's light long before it comes to brush their feathers. I can learn something from them. Even though, like the greatest teachers, they aren't teaching. Only showing how it is to love a subject. How to meet whatever comes with the music of one's being.

—JUDITH SORNBERGER

BEAR CALLS

I hear them in the early spring,
bear calls up on the side of the ridge—
a sound reminiscent of robin
but as jagged as a tree stump
gnawed by beaver.
Just yesterday, I stopped in my tracks,
certain I was hearing a long extinct bird,
or a very hoarse robin,
its call as large as a dinosaur's,
until I realized it was just another bear.
It saw me before I saw it.
This is what always happens.
Before I realize I am being blessed,
the bear turns towards its sanctuary
leaving me alone in the woods
looking up.

—FELICIA MITCHELL

THE SECRET OF LIFE

Watching my dog sleep beside me
I discover the secret of life: Air
rhythmically swells and shrinks
her whole body—a bellows
pulsing with life
inspired by air.

This ubiquitous elixir
fills our lungs, aerates our blood,
bubbles in our brain.
Asleep and awake
we ride the waves of air
as long as we live.

As long as we live we breathe
this invisible essential,
and we pass it on
one being to another
this anonymous gift
this blessing that keeps us alive.

—PATTI TANA

WINTERING

At twenty below zero in Iowa woods, the white-tailed deer live on the edge of survival. The doe lies on the brush with her young fawn nestled into her, warm breath on warm breath, heavy winter coat nudging soft spotted hide. The buck, with antlers like oak branches, stands—a sentinel—alert for the silent stalking of coyote and wolf. At evening and daybreak, the deer forage for berries—frozen past their prime, and wild shoots smothered by snow. Since each white-tail needs fourteen acres of fodder to subsist, they risk leaving the woods, wander through neighboring yards, nibble yew bushes down to the nub, chew arbor vita trees as high as their lips will reach. Instinct leads them through their winter.

Do we not, in times of ice and loss, nestle into one another, risk leaving the familiar, forage for sustenance wherever we can find it, stand like sentinels at the edges of our lives?

—DONNA WAHLERT

DEER AT SANTA SABINA

The three deer dip
their heads, take yellow
leaves into their mouths
whole, like tongues of sun.
The color feeds my eyes
as the leaves feed the deer—
the deer's bodies, the deer's eyes,
eyes that lift, dark and liquid,
and gaze into my own,
turning time spacious
and still. Together we become
one vast open eye,
life recognizing itself
inside a different skin.

We blink and the deer
go back to their leaves,
I return to my walk,
recognizing myself everywhere now—
in the moss that clings to the trees,
the stones that line the path, the sky
that arches over all of us,
eyes brimming with night,
mouth brimming with sun.

—GAYLE BRANDEIS

ALMOST AS IF

It's almost as if the catechism of earth were
written here, alchemized deep in the grain of
the poplars, in the tongue-shaped leaves of
the paper birch. Today there are only tangled vines
beneath the footpath, a hermit thrush, inventing
songs in the silence, and the swamp, half mud—
half water, dappled with sun. Above us, wild geese

veer and stretch toward the horizon, their wings
shaped to the wind. We pause to watch them dissolve
into specks on the far side of the sky's wide curve.
Circling, a hawk lifts its shadow away from the world,
and I think to myself that a Power we only begin to
understand has called us to this moment, this day, this
place in time's transept. *Nothing happens by accident.*

—ADELE KENNY

AN AFTERNOON SPENT WATCHING FLIGHTS

To know the migratory patterns of birds:
how their flight is faith, even after they lose
their way & have to circle around

Somehow it all makes sense:
this lovely gravity holding our days together
those birds, their faith—our lives

—ARLENE TRIBBIA

HUMMINGBIRD WHISPERER

Glory be to the fierce little warriors
who return to my garden every year.
Come, enjoy, drink the various nectars,
tiny bold ones. You without any fear,
teach me to cultivate fervor and focus.
Stay in our shared secret sanctuary
created for you with bergamot and phlox,
fuchsia and the feeder hung on the tree
you visit each morning. Hello! Goodbye!
Who could be freer? Fast as a torpedo
when I'm digging, spading, you catch my eye.
Faster than the wind—glanced from my window.
You share delight with your earthbound sister.
You've made me a hummingbird whisperer.

—CHRISTINE SWANBERG

A WONDERFUL MIRACLE!

Everything in Nature
is a wonderful miracle!
Isn't the little bird flying
through the big sky
a miracle?

—AMMA

EAGLES

Eagles fly over us.
Barely moving their wings

they ride the wind.
We've forgotten what we were saying

because they remind us of something
we must remember.

—SUDIE NOSTRAND

WILD GEESE

When I hear a trumpet call
From Autumn's evening sky,
I feel a quiet humility
As wild geese journey by.
It is of my mortality
I am reminded when
They signal something sacred
In another season's end.

I contemplate the message
These wild geese have implied,
That they have put their trust in one
Whose voice will be their guide,
And as I watch with reverence,
My own faith is renewed
By wild geese interrupting
My autumn solitude.

—HILDA LACHNEY SANDERSON

seven

SPIRITUALITY, PRAYERS AND BLESSINGS

Earth's crammed with heaven,
And every common bush afire with God.

—ELIZABETH BARRETT BROWNING

SACRAMENT

Take me to where cedars breathe fern
into sun-spackled afternoon.
The portable church of my bones
will fill with prayer to what lives there,
to black bears leaving claw-scribed stumps,
to lush mud exhalation of worms
to liquid throated thrush turning over moss,
to spun-wonder of spiderwebs
that catch light and make it dance.

The small bell of my heart
will be witness to this endless sacrament:
bright salmon returning from the sea
to feed the stream that spawned them,
feed the bears, those grunting dark druids,
feed the trees with whose roots bed beside water,
feed the people whose hands can not be emptied,
feed everything they touch
with the silver and rose of their beautiful flesh.

To enter here, you must put down your wristwatch
and the chatter of your cell phone and pager.
You must be willing to be small
and to be silent, like grass.

To have only your connection to the world
be your skin stroked by the wind,
your eyes washed with a hundred greens,
your ears filled with bird and water song,
the scent of cedar returning to earth all around.

—ERIN COUGHLIN HOLLOWELL

EARTH AND SPIRIT

Every step that we take upon you
should be done in a sacred manner;
each step should be
as a prayer.

—BLACK ELK

The earth I tread on is not a dead, inert mass. It is a body—has a spirit—is organic—and fluid to the influence of its spirit—and to whatever particle of that spirit is in me.

—HENRY DAVID THOREAU

O Mother Earth, You are the earthly source of all existence. The fruits which You bear are the source of life for the Earth peoples. You are always watching over Your fruits as does a mother. May the steps which we take in life upon You be sacred and not weak.

—OGLALA SIOUX PRAYER

All of creation is a symphony of joy and jubilation…
Prayer is nothing but the inhaling and exhaling of the
one breath of the universe.

—SAINT HILDEGARD OF BINGEN

There is religion in everything around us—a calm and holy religion in
the unbreathing things in nature…

—JOHN RUSKIN

The world is holy. We are holy. All life is holy. Daily prayers are
delivered on the lips of breaking waves, the whisperings of grasses, the
shimmering of leaves.

—TERRY TEMPEST WILLIAMS

Behind nature, throughout nature, spirit is present…it does not act upon us from without, that is, in space and time, but spiritually, through ourselves: therefore, that spirit, that is, the Supreme Being, does not build up nature around us, but puts forth through us, as the life of the tree puts forth new branches and leaves through the pores of old.

—RALPH WALDO EMERSON

If you wish to know the Divine,
feel the wind on your face
and the warm sun on your hand.

—THE BUDDHA

From my perspective, I absolutely believe in a greater spiritual power, far greater than I am, from which I have derived strength in moments of sadness or fear. That's what I believe, and it was very, very strong in the forest.

—JANE GOODALL

WHAT THE GOD SAYS THROUGH ME

You won't hear my poems at the poetry reading.
You won't hear my poems over the radio.
If you want what the God says through me
Come alone with me into Quetico
        and we'll canoe across lake after lake
        where there are no roads or houses
To a perfect lake with a perfect island
Where you and I will pitch our camp
        and catch fish for twilight supper.

Sitting around the fire at night
Ask me to read something I wrote
For this is the place to hear me,
More stars overhead than you ever saw,
        no other light in the woods for miles,
        no other sound but the loon
And the night wilderness smells of September.
This is the place to hear my voice
        if you want what the God says through me.

—ANTLER

FOG LIFTING

On a cool autumn morning, the earth
still wiping sleep from its eyes,
a steamy gray shroud, nestled for the night
into the bosom of a valley,
rises to shake itself out.

Hovering over green fields fresh with dew,
damp, tentative and unsure,
the veil lifts, and a rod of golden light
thrusts itself upon the land, a promise
on the tip of a magic wand.

Then, the fog lets go its grip,
yielding to fragile beauty,
and the magnificent hope of day.
Yellow light streams upon the landscape
like a sermon. Quiet prevails upon the plain.
Here, one could believe in prayer.

—ELAYNE CLIFT

ZEN GARDEN

Five dark rocks,
gray gravel raked
into circles around them.

I, who love the world,
retreat from it here.

High overhead,
light and darkness,
branches of old trees sway.

Birdsong
spills into this silence.

What can prayer be
but a small, still space
close to the city's center?

Five dark rocks, the moon rising.

—GINNY LOWE CONNORS

IN BETWEEN

I greet the morning light
with breath like fog, out
with the old, the night,
the dark, and hold
it there, the in-between,
the pause, where God
resides, before taking in
the day, what remains
to be seen. I may not
live there, but I try
to seek what is still
in the middle of living,
knowing peace only
comes like the clouds,
endless out, endless in.
In the midst of moving
we glimpse the bright
invisible within.

—CASSIE PREMO STEELE

A PEACEFUL HEART

At the center of the spiritual journey is the search for a peaceful heart. My own search began as a child, when I sometimes found peace by listening to passionate classical music or while lying in front of a fire on a winter night, staring at rushing sparks and glowing coals. It might take me by surprise on a brilliant spring afternoon when I would walk home from elementary school instead of taking the bus. Every tree, flowering bush, and blade of grass of this well-kept suburban setting seemed wonderfully, almost painfully, alive.

—ROGER S. GOTTLIEB

KNOWING GOD IS GOOD

You are a God of Love, Holy Mystery within and around us,
for your creation is crowned with the lovingness of fertile earth
and warming sun,
of insect and flower,
of workers and elders—and children.
We give thanks to be alive
and we open our hearts to an ever wider circle.
Just as nothing physical on earth is ever destroyed, only changed,
so may we have confidence
that, despite the illusions of loss and hopelessness,
our world is good,
and we are good,
and you are good.
Amen.

—WILLIAM CLEARY

RESPLENDENT WORLD

God, you love our earth; from sunrise to sunset
you fill land and sea with riches;
the hills rejoice at your touch;
the valleys shout for joy,
they sing.
Open our eyes to this resplendent world
that we may care for the earth
as our companion in creation.

May the pure song of air, water, and trees
broaden our minds,
lift up our hearts, and guide us to you.

—STACY BRADLEY

A PRAYER FOR WISDOM

Let me be free enough to dwell amongst the tangle
to seek the pathways overgrown
to shun the human need for construct
and refining all that's wild
Let me be bold enough to revel in the mystery of chaos
to see the beauty in the overlap
and relinquish the ordering of pieces
in a fool's quest for control
Let me be faithful enough to surrender to uncertainty
to trust what only nature knows
and set aside the need for naming
and claiming all I've named
Let me walk barefoot amongst the thorns
and risk the prick to feel the brush of leaves
so I may come to my carpet with muddy feet
and a mind reeling with precious secrets of the woods

—LISA POJE ANGELOS

TO EARTH

Oh, Earth, swirling blue planet,
work of a conscious and consummate creator,
and holding in balance rich fertile loam
the breath of the atmosphere
swelling seas and steady surf.
Be patient with us faltering caretakers.
Forgive the soiling of banks of clay, brows of hills
global waters and cosmic air.
You are speaking to us in flood and drought
winds and temblors and quakes.
Teach us, sweet earth, that you have limits
to your plentitude, adaptation, and endurance.
Let us rediscover your nobility, fragility
tenderness and sacredness.

—DONNA WAHLERT

INVOCATION

Mother Earth, it is not you
who needs to be invoked—
for you are always here!
But we your human children
who today must be invoked—
who have abandoned you, forgotten
to call upon you, neglected to care for you,
failed to serve you and disregarded your needs.
Help us now to awaken and remember
our obligations to you and all Earth's beings.
Let your spirit fill us with love, appreciation, joy
and overwhelming desire to serve you in all that we do.
May we think and speak and act as one family of one Mother
who gives life to all and when it is time, takes it away.

Guide us, Great Mother, in every decision we make,
every habit we develop, every action we undertake.
May we never forget you again, beloved Mother Earth,
beautiful and bountiful source and resting place and wonder.

—JANINE CANAN

ALL PRAISE BE YOURS

All praise be yours, my Lord, through all that you have made,
And first my Lord *Brother Sun,*
Who brings the day; and light you give to us through him.
How beautiful is he, how radiant in all his splendor.
Of you, Most High, he bears the likeness.

And praise be yours, my Lord, through *Sister Moon*
and stars; in the heavens you have made them bright,
and precious, and fair.

All praise be yours, my Lord, through *Sister Earth,*
Our Mother, who feeds us in her sovereignty and
produces fruits and colored flowers and herbs.

—SAINT FRANCIS OF ASSISI

DOXOLOGY

The heavens are thine,
the earth also is thine

—PSALM 89:11

Holy, the heavens
Holy, the earth
Holy, the spirit
Holy, what breathes
Holy, the daily
Holy abstractions
Holy, each minute
Holy unceasing
Holy creation
Holy Creator
Holy, what's lost
Holy, what's found
Holy, the Whole

—MARYANNE HANNAN

INVOCATION FOR THE EARTH

Dear Creator, please join us today as we honor our home, this blue-green Earth, forever circling the dwarf yellow star we call the Sun, blessed with resources essential for life—pure air, fertile land, sweet water, edible plants—if we live responsibly, realizing our actions, as small as using and discarding plastic bags, as immense as shearing mountains to harvest coal and damming rivers running free—impact its future.

Sometimes the Earth must groan under the weight of our greed and selfishness, our blindness to its beauty and its fragility. So we gather here to remember that to be good and faithful stewards of our environment requires constant vigilance, that the preservation of its well-being requires strength and sacrifice as well as the belief that all children deserve exactly what we want for ours—drinking a glass of water with no worry, planting a garden, frolicking in the sea, going to bed every night without hunger.

Bless us today as we work to revere and protect the Earth and all its life.

—SUZANNE C. COLE

THE BLESSING OF LIGHT

May the blessing of light be on you,
light without and light within.

May the blessed sunlight shine upon you
and warm your heart
till it glows like a great fire
and strangers may warm themselves
as well as friends.

And may the light shine out of the eyes of you,
like a candle set in the window of a house,
bidding the wanderer to come in
out of the storm.

May the blessing of rain be on you,
the soft sweet rain.
May it fall upon your spirit
so that little flowers may spring up
and shed their sweetness on the air.

And may the blessing of the great rains be on you,
to beat upon your spirit and wash it fair and clean;
and leave there many a shining pool
where the blue of heaven shines,
and sometimes a star.

May the blessing of the earth be on you,
the great round earth.

May you ever have a kindly greeting for people
as you're going along the roads.

And now may the Lord bless you,
and bless you kindly. Amen.

—AUTHOR UNKNOWN

eight

JOY, PRAISE
AND GRATITUDE

Oh Matchless Earth—
We underrate the chance to dwell in thee.

—EMILY DICKINSON

JUST ANOTHER DAY

It's just another doughnut day in the universe.
I want to smash my face into flour, fluff, and sweetness
and forget anything that prevents me from feeling
the absolute joy of birdsong or yellow balloon
whether it be deadline or telephone line
the electronic busyness of our lives
for there are rows of tulips conspiring pink
and lovers breathless next to willow trees.
There are lilacs whispering among their twisted trunks
and windmills whirling through Van Gogh's ear.
There is color everywhere
and sprinkles of hope in my heart
that you will feel the freedom
of renegade rivers and the vast expanse
of starry starry nights.
Connect the dots, the body of water
between us, this great flood of love
that seeps through and beyond the earth.

—TERRI GLASS

JUST THERE

The way the trees beside this road
lift their branches into rain,
just there against the cloudy sky,
tells me they are glad to be
still blossoming, though they are old.

Last night in the sunset,
I saw the newborn leaves of one
light up like celery and give themselves
to a small wind, and I bowed my head
in that light.

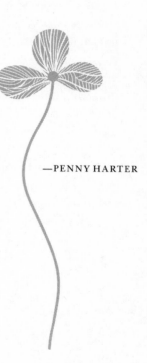

—PENNY HARTER

PRAISE SONG

Praise the light of late November,
even though there's been another tragedy,
a plane crash, all passengers lost. Praise
the thin sunlight that goes deep in the bones.
Praise the crows chattering in the oak trees;
though they are clothed in night, they do not despair.
Praise what little there's left: the small boats
of milkweed pods, husks, hulls, shells,
the architecture of trees. Praise the meadow
of dried weeds: yarrow, goldenrod, chicory,
the remains of summer. Praise the blue sky
that hasn't cracked. Praise the sun slipping down
behind the beechnuts, praise the quilt of leaves
that covers the grass: Scarlet Oak, Liquidambar,
Sugar Maple. Though darkness gathers, praise
our crazy fallen world; it's all we have, and it's never enough.

—BARBARA CROOKER

A NEW DOXOLOGY

Praise God
>   praise goodness

from Whom
>   from where

all blessings flow
>   like rivers, rain,
>   and winds that blow

praise Him, all creatures here below
>   mosquito, sparrow, buffalo

praise Him above
>   praise Creation everywhere

ye heavenly host
>   in starry sky
>   and starfish on the beach

praise Father, Son, and Holy Ghost
>   praise each woman, man and child,
>   fertile Earth and all things wild.

—BARBARA LYDECKER CRANE

ON EARTH

Morning—
so quiet.

I place my hand on woven carpet—
the lambs gave their wool.

Underneath, the floor—
the oaks gave their bark.

Below, cement—
the land gave her sands.

Good Morning, dear,
I greet the living Earth.

—JANINE CANAN

A DANCE

I dance on the earth
my long legs reach down
to the soft ground;
I am fed by secret rivers;

I move with the moon
my tree-filled arms
could almost touch the sky;
Stars fill my dreams.

I stop dancing
only to sleep
when the blanket of night
protects me.

—PAMELA L. LASKIN

EARTH SONG

All the earth echoes a grateful song
From mountains high to rivers long.
Forests and prairies, flowers and trees,
Mighty winds, the peaceful breeze,

Each tiny pebble, each waterfall voice
In silence and song lives to rejoice.
And so, we, too, our hymn we raise
Joining creation's chorus of praise.

—THERESA MARY GRASS

THANK YOU, THANK YOU

It's simple, it's easy, we just pray
Thank you, thank you, thank you
For blessing us with this blue sky day
With all heaven's gifts shining down upon us

—GARY E. MCCORMICK

WALKING ALONE ON A THICKLY STARRED NIGHT

to the ringing of crickets, the bullfrog's
thrumming bass: the whole earth
is vibrating, singing.
This is a walk on the skin of things,
listening to the pulse, as the dust & swirl
of the Milky Way dance overhead,
and I walk past black trees
that are the shadows of trees,
so dark that the edge of the world
might be one step ahead,
but always the Dipper is tilting, rising over
the black cathedral of pines, always points
the way back home.

—BARBARA CROOKER

BENEDICTE AMERICA—
A CANTICLE OF CREATION

Let all creation sing God's praise,
glorify God with thanksgiving and praise.

1 O sun and moon, you stars of the western skies,
  all daybreak and sunset, twilight and noon;
Lightning and snow storm, fire and wind,
  thunder and rainbow, geyser and spark;
Let all creation sing God's praise
Glorify God with thanksgiving and praise.

2 You maple and pine trees, oak and palmetto,
  seedling and lichen, flower and weed;
All mountains and valleys, canyon and plain,
  caverns, wheat fields, deserts, and rocks;
Let all creation sing God's praise
Glorify God with thanksgiving and praise.

3 You rainfall and rivers, you oceans and ponds,
  all tides and marshes, coastland and dune;
Porpoise and dolphin, starfish and shark,
  sea urchins, sandpipers, cowrie and shrimp;
Let all creation sing God's praise
Glorify God with thanksgiving and praise.

4   You horses and lizards, you spiders and dogs,
        badger, mouse, hedgehog, owl and hawk;
    All beaver and heron, kitfox and crane,
        muskrats, bumblebees, turtle, and bat;
    Let all creation sing God's praise
    Glorify God with thanksgiving and praise.

5   You prophets and sages, you martyrs and mystics,
        saints of the cities, the hills and the towns;
    All babies and children, all women and men,
        all pilgrims, and lovers, all seekers of truth;
    Let all creation sing God's praise
    Glorify God with thanksgiving and praise.

6   You singers and dancers, all potters and poets,
        artist, and writer, and dreamer of dreams;
    All color and light, all movement and sound,
        all silence and waking, all feeling and thought;
    Let all creation sing God's praise
    Glorify God with thanksgiving and praise.

—REVEREND ANNE KELSEY

BOREAL REVEAL

You can not know the night
when you'll be walking the dogs,
boots shattering the snow
as you watch the ground
for slick places that might
carry you away from yourself,
while above, all unnoticed
the light gathers together
writhing for your pleasure
and you look for the source
of the hiss that begins to sift
through the trees, and there
across the dark stage of the sky
is the eternal waltz revealed.
Oh the swirl of mysterious skirts
catches your breath
and you
fall.

—ERIN COUGHLIN HOLLOWELL

COMMUNION

(Excerpt from *Gone Wild*)

Christmas afternoon, snow came down in gauze sheets, reminding me of fiber that swaddles something fine. A newborn soul. Or a dazzling trinket in a little box. Time spent in nature, I thought, would be the best part of my holiday, and I savored unwrapping the gift. I opened the car door, and my dog Dewey and I entered a world of trees and frozen water, where the only sound was of ever-so-light flakes drifting down and touching snow. Here, within mere miles of jets roaring down runways, there were, for a time, no artificial sounds: not a car engine whirring, a bus's brakes shrieking or a stereo's woofers thrumming. Even the wheeze of my breath was muffled by the curtain of snow and sky, meshed into something like velvet. In this tableau, there were no other players, just Dewey—his snout deliberately seeking a scent in the fresh powder—and me, in mukluks, feet palpitating the earth.

The precipitation, the clouds, the coated tree limbs, the ice floes on the river, were all different shades of white. Not even a dog's yellow graffiti marred the spotless surface. I was getting a much-needed dose of solitude, silence. It felt holy—way beyond church—this communion, for me. My footfalls sang a hymn as I entrained with the surroundings, praising this place I come to often. Familiarity expanded my vision, the way ritual does, repeating the mundane until it becomes again a mystery.

—MILISSA LINK

EARTH DAY

The dog calls me out of sleep.
Overnight the wind has rearranged
everything. I blow into cold hands
and raise them against the sun's
first rays, just now
exploding gold shrapnel
over the east ridge.

And everything is moving, sun
shattered through the new green
leaves, and wind plucking
overnight spider-webs, gold filaments
against the dark trunks of oaks,
everything flowing glowing
gold-green, a morning

no mortal could describe.
And so my dog stands
simply wagging. Wasn't he good
to bring me here?

—TAYLOR GRAHAM

HERE BY THE WATER

Soft field of clover
Moon shining over the valley
Joining the song of the river
To the great Giver
Of the great good

As it enfolds me
Somehow it holds me together
I realize I've been singing
Still it comes ringing
Clearer than clear

And here by the water
I'll build an altar to praise you
Out of the stones that I've found here
I'll set them down here
Rough as they are
Knowing you can make them holy

—JIM CROEGAERT

RETURNING THANKS

We return thanks to our mother, the earth,
which sustains us.
We return thanks to the rivers and streams,
which supply us with water.
We return thanks to all herbs,
which furnish medicines for the cure of our diseases.
We return thanks to the moon and stars,
which have given to us their light when the sun was gone.
We return thanks to the sun,
that has looked upon the earth with a beneficent eye.
Lastly, we return thanks to the Great Spirit,
in Whom is embodied all goodness,
and Who directs all things for the good of Her children.

—IROQUOIS PRAYER

THANKFULNESS

Let us thank the Earth
That offers ground for home
And holds our feet firm

—JOHN O'DONOHUE

the mountains and hills will burst into song
…all the trees of the field will clap their hands!

—ISAIAH 55:12 (NLT)

Each day, I will bless
and evermore sing praise.

—MARCIA FALK

When we live in harmony with nature
The earth sings out in gratitude.

—BARB MAYER

A TOAST TO MORNING

As morning broke its egg upon the slopes and the land became washed by yellow, orange and white rivulets of light, I felt as though I was watching a finely choreographed drama in which the sky spoke to the contours of the mountains, and the breeze to the trill of songbirds among the leaves. The air was thick with the plot of a story that was waking up from night's adventures. I sing a paean to nature because nature sings to me.

—RAMNATH SUBRAMANIAN

O CREATOR

You, O Creator, have formed our world in beauty.
Your gentle spirit
whispered our names,
and we were born,
called to share the promise of earth
and, yes, the universe.
We are one with you,
as with all creation
we praise you,
we glorify you,
we thank you.

—THERESA MARY GRASS

HERITAGE

Great Mother Earth
I am the fruit of your womb
along with the grace of green things growing,
azure rush of water and electric song of stormy sky
Great Mother Gaia
I too am the child of your love
like the panther and the dove,
rainbow trout leaping for joy in an April stream
or summer's last firefly
Great Goddess of the seasons:
guardian of dark and light,
I am born of your balance,
blessed by this Mystery of life

—ARLENE GAY LEVINE

TUGGING US TOWARD WONDER

Tugging toward wonder,
everything grows
imperceptibly upward,

the earth turns, animals migrate
and chance invites us to the dance
as we move across fields

that both flower and fade
as if we had gathered at the table
of this shared universe

simply to look at the invitation
of each other's eyes,
offer grace

and notice something wondrous,
waiting to be embraced.

—MICHAEL S. GLASER

LIFE IS PRECIOUS

God of Everything,
if life is precious,
earth is precious and every part of it.
Should we not thank you continuously
for the very air surrounding our planet?
Should we not thank you for the fertile soil
we plow up and cultivate,
for the rain storms that sweep across it and enliven it,
for every single burgeoning seed and bud and leaf?
We also thank you for our own greatest liveliness:
our limitless yearning for life which may be the very force of
    evolution.
We give thanks now and always.
Amen.

—WILLIAM CLEARY

LISTEN,

I want to tell you something. This morning
is bright after all the steady rain, and every iris,
peony, rose, opens its mouth, rejoicing. I want to say,
wake up, open your eyes, there's a snow-covered road
ahead, a field of blankness, a sheet of paper, an empty screen.
Even the smallest insects are singing, vibrating their entire bodies,
tiny violins of longing and desire. We were made for song.
I can't tell you what prayer is, but I can take the breath
of the meadow into my mouth, and I can release it for the leaves'
green need. I want to tell you your life is a blue coal, a slice
of orange in the mouth, cut hay in the nostrils. The cardinals'
red song dances in your blood. Look, every month the moon
blossoms into a peony, then shrinks to a sliver of garlic.
And then it blooms again.

—BARBARA CROOKER

THE THIRD BEATITUDE

Blessed was I today for I did inherit the earth
and the earth was constant and miraculous.
The winter wind chatted with the wind chimes
and was my morning wake-up call.
The hills wrapped themselves in resplendent ermine
and I walked among them with reflected elegance.
The air was laundered and crisply starched
and crinkled and crackled in my nose and lungs.
A sparrow danced about the hawthorn in a lively fandango
and I clapped my hands and shouted ole, ole!
Blessed was I today for I did inherit the earth
and the earth was constant and miraculous.

—SUSAN J. ERICKSON

nine
REFLECTIONS

What is the need of Heaven
When earth can be so sweet?

—EDNA ST. VINCENT MILLAY

THE CADENCE OF EARTH

the throb of the heart
in earth's central fire

the thrum of the ocean
as it washes ashore

this the pulsation
of life in my lungs

the rhythm that sings
through time and through space

this is the drum
that plays in my veins

this beating of earth
that rings to the stars

—JOANNA M. WESTON

PRESENCE

Through my experience with lakes and forests I began to change to a view of the body as earth. The streambeds, I knew, were surfaces of life. They spoke to me, as did the great mountains and towering trees that cycled and used the waters around me. From streams and forests and mountains I felt excitement, beauty, inspiration. Where did these feelings come from? I first assumed that such feelings arose inside myself, from a chamber somewhere in my heart or mind. On thinking about it, however, I came to realize that my imagination and feelings were aroused not by self-generation alone, but because the earth was somehow communicating with me. The soil—the earth as a whole— had presence.

—TOM HAYDEN

FIND A PLACE ON EARTH

Once in awhile you find a place on earth that becomes your very own.
A place undefined. Waiting for you to bring your color, your self. A
place untouched, unspoiled, undeveloped. Raw, honest, and haunting.
No one, nothing is telling you how to feel or who to be. Let the
mountains have you for a day...

—SUNDANCE

THIS EARTH DESERVES YOU

You are sitting on the earth, and you realize that this earth deserves
you and you deserve this earth. You are there—fully, personally,
genuinely.

—CHOGYUM TRUNGPA

WHATEVER BEFALLS THE EARTH

Every part of this earth is sacred to my people. Every shining pine needle, every sandy shore, every mist in the dark woods, every clearing and every humming insect is holy in the memory and experience of my people.

Whatever befalls the earth befalls the sons of the earth. Man did not weave the web of life; he is merely a strand in it. Whatever he does to the web, he does to himself. How can you buy or sell the sky? The warmth of the land? The idea is strange to us. If we do not own the freshness of the air and the sparkle of the water, how can you buy them?

—CHIEF SEATTLE

TREAT THE EARTH WELL

Treat the earth well.
It was not given to you by your parents,
it was loaned to you by your children.
We do not inherit the Earth from our Ancestors,
we borrow it from our Children.

—NATIVE AMERICAN PROVERB

THE MEASURE OF A CIVILIZATION

I do not think the measure of a civilization
is how tall its buildings of concrete are,
but rather how well its people have learned to relate
to their environment and fellow man.

—SUN BEAR OF THE CHIPPEWA TRIBE

PESSIMISTIC OR OPTIMISTIC?

When asked if I am pessimistic or optimistic about the future, my
answer is always the same: If you look at the science about what is
happening on earth and aren't pessimistic, you don't understand data.
But if you meet the people who are working to restore this earth and
the lives of the poor, and you aren't optimistic, you haven't got a pulse.

—PAUL HAWKEN

COME TO MEET

Today,
I need the silence
of the breeze,
the company
of birds singing,
the comfort
of water upon rocks.

Today,
I need the earth
to let me sit and be,
the smell of trees and leaves,
a flower and a seed.

Today,
I need you nature
to be there and not be,
to be the silent witness
of an encounter between—
my Creator and me.

—ZORAIDA RIVERA MORALES

EARTH, TEACH ME

Earth, teach me stillness
  as the grasses are stilled with light.
Earth, teach me suffering
  as old stones suffer with memory.
Earth, teach me humility
  as blossoms are humble with beginning.
Earth, teach me caring
  as the mother who secures her young.
Earth, teach me courage
  as the tree that stands all alone.
Earth, teach me limitation
  as the ant that crawls on the ground.
Earth, teach me freedom
  as the eagle that soars in the sky.
Earth, teach me resignation
  as the leaves that die in the fall.
Earth, teach me regeneration
  as the seed that rises in the spring.
Earth, teach me to forget myself
  as melted snow forgets its life.
Earth, teach me to remember kindness
  as dry fields weep with rain.

—UTE PRAYER

A GREEN SOMEWHERE

Somewhere exists a virgin rain forest—
great green trees stretching to pure skies,
trunks and branches dripping with epiphytes—
stubby lichen, hanging mosses, sturdy vines—
and adorned with birds—toucans, perhaps
iridescent hummingbirds or scarlet macaws,
their song interlaced with the sound of
moisture—clouds condensing and dewfall—
slowly trickling downward to mingle
with braided streams ambling towards the sea.
Monkeys call and clamber through the canopy
above a sloth suspended from an angled branch,
all breathing a purer air than I will ever know.

If humans have traversed here,
their passage has left no mark—
no campfire scars, no Styrofoam,
no soap scum to sully the landscape.
This forest by me may be unvisited,
forever only a green somewhere,
but my soul, assaulted by industrial roar,
half-sick with posturing politicians—
needs to know such wilderness exists.

—SUZANNE C. COLE

GREEN

It is good to be near green:
sweet grass growing even through concrete,
leaves in every conceivable design
gracing oak or rose or vine, peaceful pastures
where cradled in emerald you can surrender
to the sky all regrets and worries of Time.

It is healing to be near green:
to be swathed in the incense of growing things
a scent both fresh and ancient,
to follow the stream weaving
through deep forest to the heart
of the evergreen cathedral
sculpted stone by stone
from the days and ways of your life
purring greenly there in the silence
like the prayer that it is.

—ARLENE GAY LEVINE

NO ONE OWNS A TREE

No one truly owns a tree—it is the gift of a moment
to the passerby who pauses to admire
its crown of gold in late September, a place of rest
to all the generations as they climb
into its generous embrace. A tree belongs to the birds
that make their home among its boughs
and to everyone who lingers in its shade
searching for glimpses of heaven
caught by its breath-giving branches.

—EMILY RUTH HAZEL

I AM COMING BACK AS A TREE

When I die, she said, I am coming back as a tree with deep roots and
I'll wave my leaves to the children every morning on their way to
school & whisper tree songs at night in their dreams. Trees with deep
roots know about the things that children need.

—BRIAN ANDREAS

THE PATH

Walking down the path in the dark,
only the glow of a fading flashlight,
I hear the sound of waves hitting rock.

It's almost midnight and dew covers everything,
the sky is peppered with stars.
Fireflies throw themselves across the ground
like sparks;

a breeze builds to a rushing wind;
specks of silver
are scattered across a seamless piece of unending dark blue.

Except for crickets
there is silence;
no view except night sky.
And my mind races.

In this tiny place on earth
while I stand thinking,
soft animals move across mountains.

—MAGIE DOMINIC

CHORUS OF STARS

Everything lives, moves, everything corresponds; the magnetic rays, emanating either from myself or from others, cross the limitless chain of created things unimpeded; it is a transparent network that covers the world, and its slender threads communicate themselves by degrees to the planets and stars. Captivate now upon the earth, I commune with the chorus of the stars who share in my joys and sorrows.

—GÉRARD DE NERVAL

I CARE SO MUCH ABOUT THE EARTH

I've flown over New Zealand's hanging glaciers
and walked to and touched the icy blue of others
that flow into their own azure melt as thick as milk.
I've cruised the Norwegian fjords
entering their sacred crevices and waterfalls.

I've lunched on bread and cheese on the Matterhorn
and listened to the bells of the cows below
as they rang in praise of the Swiss Alps.
I've sat in awe at the rim of the Grand Canyon
with its orange and red and ochre layers
that only God could have carved and colored.

I care so much about the earth.

I've swum in the coral of the Great Barrier reef;
and floated on a barge that slowly ruffled
the canal waters of the Marne river—
sampling French cheeses from countryside herds
tasting the champagnes from vineyards
that flamboyantly run down to the shore.

And what will we do when the bergs of ice melt,
the waters rise and wash away the vineyards and shores;
and fill the fjords and silence the jangling cow bells
and bury the multi-colored ledges of the canyons?
Will those that survive, ages from now, sit
and wait as crests ebb and another dove returns
with another olive branch?

Oh, I care so much about the earth.

—DONNA WAHLERT

ONE SUMMER NIGHT

I sat on my deck and watched the evening come.
Birds called softly from their roosts.
A slight breeze brought the scent of pine.
Overhead, on the black cloth of night,
pin points glistened in the moon's pale gleam.
Insect harmonies filled the air
singing praise to the Creator.
My heart joined in.

—CINDY BREEDLOVE

LISTEN TO THE SOUNDS

Shh. Listen to the sounds that surround you. Notice the pitches, the
volume, the timbre, the many lines of counterpoint. As light taught
Monet to paint, the earth may be teaching you music.

—PETE SEEGER

LISTEN

to the small music of the summer rain, its vertical
green stanzas, the swish of tires, as cars push up
the sloping road, leaving silence in their wake.
How inured we are to constant sound, how seldom
do we dwell in silence, brew a cup of tea. Blue lobelia
overflows in hanging baskets over the white porch railing;
rain fills the gutters, filters through maple leaves,
drips in the cedars, makes sequins of droplets
on lilies of the valley. This deep green space:
tire music, water music, bird song in the interstices.
What seeps in the earth returns to the sky,
a brimful pot of flowers, a blue cascade of stars.

—BARBARA CROOKER

SUMMER EVENING WITH KAYAK

A single kayak drifts
for a moment, into the middle
of a meditation. Across the lake
a dog barks three times and then

falls silent. Tonight the green
waters seem very still. Fish rise
into silk circles that pattern
the lake's calm surface.

Clouds, underlit, take
on the colors of summer fruits.
The tops of trees are still bright.
The sun's dipped past the horizon

and for the man in his narrow boat,
ordinary life has slipped away too.
His paddle rests on his knees.
Swallows skim over the water.

From the shore I watch the kayaker
glide silently out beyond me
but I know somehow
that our minds have drifted

into the same timeless space.
You do not have to belong
to any church. You do not have
to prostrate yourself or fling coins

in the direction of redemption.
Just let yourself drift sometimes
unhurried, unwanting.
Something like this will find you.

—GINNY LOWE CONNORS

REFLECTIONS ON THE EARTH

All living things are interwoven
each with the other; the tie is sacred.

—MARCUS AURELIUS

The earth is not a mere fragment of dead history, stratum upon
stratum like the leaves of a book, to be studied by geologists and
antiquarians chiefly, but living poetry like the leaves of a tree, which
precede flowers and fruit—not a fossil earth, but a living earth.

—HENRY DAVID THOREAU

Those who contemplate the beauty of the earth
find reserves of strength that will endure as long as life lasts.

—RACHEL CARSON

You are a meeting place of gravitation and grace...
You have something of the earth and something of the sky within you.

—OSHO

I said in my heart,
"I am sick of four walls and a ceiling.
I have need of the sky.
I have business with the grass."

—RICHARD HOVEY

We are all wanderers on this earth—
our hearts are full of wonder
and our souls are deep with dreams.

—GYPSY PROVERB

There are times when we stop. We sit still…
We listen and breezes from a whole other world
begin to whisper.

—JAMES CARROLL

Around us, life bursts forth with miracles—a glass of water, a ray of sunshine, a leaf, a caterpillar, a flower, laughter, raindrops.

—THICH NHAT HANH

The world is full of poetry.
The air is living with its spirit,
And the waves dance to the music of its melodies,
And sparkle in its brightness.

—JAMES GATES PERCIVAL

All is miracle. The stupendous order of nature, the revolution of a hundred millions of worlds around a million of suns, the activity of light, the life of animals, all are grand and perpetual miracles.

—VOLTAIRE

ten

MAKING CHANGES

To love the earth
is to love our home.

—JUNE COTNER

WORKING TOGETHER

Comfort the Earth with gardens
of every shape and size
Soothe its bruises
with all variations of fragrance
and colorful designs
Invite birds in to visit
and share joyous songs
Offer the patient
refreshing drinks of water
and vitamin-rich compost
Dig constantly
to awaken Earth to new vigor
Let your busy hands
transfer love and caring
from seed to root
to budding plant
Together, you and Earth
can heal the wounds,
stop the pain,
banish the illness of neglect.

—SHEILA FORSYTH

BUILDING A COMPOST PILE

is not unlike building a poem: making something
out of nothing, turning straw into gold, garbage into loam.
Take what others would throw out:
eggshells, apple peels, coffee grounds,
newspapers full of cumbersome verbiage,
banana skins, grapefruit rinds, grass clippings,
and add to it daily.

If it seems like nothing's happening, you're wrong.
In the dark, heat and pressure build;
things begin to break down, add up.
Turn, aerate, let it breathe. Add water.
Add worms. Add eye of newt, and bacteria.

It's earthy as a river; it smells like a stable floor.
Are those critics I hear, typing away,
or crickets in the corner of the woodpile?
How do you know when it's done?
Well, you don't, you just abandon it,
to misquote Paul Valéry.

But scoop some out—moist and dark as a chocolate torte,
black gold; this compost, this humus, it's a richness
you can never get enough of.

—BARBARA CROOKER

TO FRANK MICHLER CHAPMAN

My dear Mr. Chapman:

I need hardly say how heartily I sympathize with the purposes of the Audubon Society. I would like to see all harmless wild things, but especially all birds protected in every way. I do not understand how any man or woman who really loves nature can fail to try to exert all influence in support of such objects as those of the Audubon Society. Spring would not be spring without bird songs, any more than it would be spring without buds and flowers, and I only wish that besides protecting the songsters, the birds of the grove, the orchard, the garden and the meadow, we could also protect the birds of the sea shore and of the wilderness. The loon ought to be, and, under wise legislation, could be a feature of every Adirondack lake; ospreys, as everyone knows, can be made the tamest of the tame; and terns should be as plentiful along our shores as swallows around our barns. A tanager or a cardinal makes a point of glowing beauty in the green woods, and the cardinal among the white snows. When the bluebirds were so nearly destroyed by the severe winter a few seasons ago, the loss was like the loss of an old friend, or at least like the burning down of a familiar and dearly loved house. How immensely it would add to our forests if only the great logcock were still found among them! The destruction of the wild pigeon and the Carolina paraquet has meant a loss as severe as if the Catskills or the Palisades were taken away. When

I hear of the destruction of a species I feel just as if all the works of some great writer had perished; as if we had lost all instead of only part of Polybius or Livy.

Very truly yours,
—THEODORE ROOSEVELT

PERSPECTIVE

Think for today.
Act for tomorrow.

—BARB MAYER

When all the trees have been cut down,
when all the animals have been hunted,
when all the waters are polluted,
when all the air is unsafe to breathe,
only then will you discover you cannot eat money.

—CREE PROPHECY

When you drink the water,
remember the well.

—CHINESE PROVERB

Don't eat anything your great-grandmother
wouldn't recognize as food.

—MICHAEL POLLAN

From a tree-planting volunteer: "There's an old saying that you don't get to sleep under the shade of the tree you plant. That's fine. I think I owe something back, even if I don't see the benefit."

—BILL WASSON

All of us are accountable, responsible and ultimately powerful when it comes to the future for life on Earth. The most dangerous adversary to conservation is a sense of being helpless or powerless. No matter what your age is, or your economic standing, we all can make a difference.

—JEFF CORWIN

Our goal is not just an environment of clean air and water and scenic beauty. The objective is an environment of decency, quality and mutual respect for all other human beings and all other living creatures.

—GAYLORD NELSON

A BAREFOOT BLESSING

My yoga instructor tells me
To root down into the earth.
Feel the earth's energy and
Draw it up into your being.
All I feel is pain and sorrow.
The earth hurts, and so do I.
Drained and dark, thick and heavy,
Choking, clogging, weighted down.
The time has come to tread lightly.
No more digging, poking, pain.
Only softness, walking barefoot.
Little children...light again.
Giving the earth breathing space,
Blowing healing air onto its wounds.
Who is Mother Earth's mother?
Hush, hush...rest now.
Always doing, time for being.
Be beautiful, and I'll be gentle.
Ever tiptoeing towards home.

—CHERYL PAULSON

NATURAL CURE

The best remedy for those who are afraid, lonely or unhappy is to go outside, somewhere where they can be quiet, alone with the heavens, nature and God. Because only then does one feel that all is as it should be and that God wishes to see people happy, amidst the simple beauty of nature.

—ANNE FRANK

GO TAKE A HIKE!

Go take a hike! Backpacking is the cheapest of vacations, and it links you intimately and directly to the world around you. It reminds us that we are just a part of the natural order, not lord of it, and that humble acknowledgment is the first step to improve our stewardship.

—NICHOLAS D. KRISTOF

LET US PRESS FORWARD

Let us press forward. Let us resolve to conduct ourselves in such a way that our children's children will read about the "Spirit of Kyoto," and remember well the place and the time where humankind first chose to embark together on a long-term sustainable relationship between our civilization and the Earth's environment.

In that spirit, let us transcend our differences and commit to secure our common destiny: a planet whole and healthy, whose nations are at peace, prosperous and free; and whose people everywhere are able to reach for their God-given potential.

—AL GORE

EARTH DAY

O God of whirling galaxies, rain forests and rivers, tides and thunderstorms, we've been too busy to notice how our choices affect our world. At last we're paying attention: You gave us a gift but we were careless and now it's broken. We gather today, repentant, hopeful, and determined to restore, cleanse, and bring new life to earth, wind, and creature. Let us share Your imagination; let us be Your fingers as we tend this gift, which holds and carries us all.

—REVEREND J. LYNN JAMES

DO NOT DIVERT YOUR LOVE

Do not divert your love from visible things.
But go on loving what is good, simple and ordinary;
animals and things and flowers,
and keep the balance true.

—RAINER MARIA RILKE

eleven
INSPIRATION

Walk as if you were kissing
the earth with your feet.

—THICH NHAT HANH

THE RESONANCE AROUND US

As we walk through this field, coarse grasses
vibrate around our ankles. Listen, we are already
in the sky, its rising glissando trembling in the
hollows of our bones—our bones that might be
wind chimes hanging from the trees, clattering
like a hard rain.

Tonight it will snow, each crystal a tuning fork
for the other, each of our upturned faces echoing
the quiet ticking flakes that home on us.

Even those things we deem silent—dead weeds
nodding by the barn, the piles the horses drop
as they drift through the pasture, steam rising
from each before it cools—even these
are singing in their spheres.

Listen, and you might hear the choir of atoms,
those unseen constellations that make flesh,
flickering on and off as they resonate with
the dead who float beside us, their substance
oscillating faster than we apprehend.

Just now some bird that knows the notes
of twilight opened its beak to offer a brief
harmony, and as the dark descends in solemn
chords, a chorus of plum clouds begins to hum
on Earth's horizon.

—PENNY HARTER

SAYS MOTHER EARTH

My child, put your head on my softness
Let my warmth soothe your scars
Let my rain wash your tears
Let my wind waft your prayers
up and over the farthest mountain
Take now this moment
the breath I give you
the breath I will receive
You are mine
I am yours

—MARYANNE HANNAN

PRAYER FOR THE CITY

In the world I hope for,
trains run on schedule
and people have time
to smile in passing
instead of simply pushing,
frantic, unseeing,
through the exhaust fumes
of their scattered days.

I long to live in the heart of
possibility, in a place
that smells like eucalyptus,
in a city with no sirens.
There, no one has to beg
to be human; everyone
has clean socks, a warm bed
where it is safe to sleep;
and on each roof
a garden breathes.

—EMILY RUTH HAZEL

ONE

Open the door a little more,
feast your eyes on the skies,
the wonder, the glory,
the sweet endless story
of all that is sacred and wise.

Within us,
without us,
above us, below,
the journey, the ebb,
the answer, the flow,

the earth, the sea,
the stars and the sky
tell us the tale of the sparrow and whale
of the who and the where
and the why.

Nothing begins,
nothing is done,
the present, the past,
and future
are one.

—CHARLES GHIGNA

A POEM FOR PEACE

I have watched herons
standing one-legged
on the shores of long brown rivers.
I have drifted past
the reflections of stars
on lakes deep with silence.

And high in the mountains
I have seen ancient drawings
carved into stones
by the people who came before us.
Everything they knew
cannot have vanished.

Within me I carry
the sunlight and the stars,
the image of a red fox
trotting past long grasses
on the side of a road
just as the moon is setting.

I know the eyes of a lover,
the cries of a newborn,
the wishes of a greedy child.
And I am that lover,
that newborn,
that child wanting everything.

Let us listen to the music of stars
as mountains do. Let us go
together to the edge of a lake
as the clouds turn violet and gold,
let us watch the moose turn
graceful in water. Let us bow down to it.

—GINNY LOWE CONNORS

THE ONE GREAT SECRET

Human beings—any one of us, and our species as a whole—are not all-important, not at the center of the world. That is the one essential piece of information, the one great secret, offered by any encounter with the woods or the mountains or the ocean or any wilderness or chunk of nature or patch of night sky.

—BILL MCKIBBEN

I PLEDGE ALLEGIANCE

I pledge allegiance to the Earth,
and all the Life which it supports,
one planet in our care,
irreplaceable,
with sustenance and respect for all.

—AUTHOR UNKNOWN

LOVELY EARTH

Lovely Earth,
We call you Mother.
You have carried us in your warm swaling womb.
You have charted in your body everything we need to sustain life.
You have furnished us with waters, plants, fruits to nourish us
and the very air we breathe has been blest.
You forged coal and oil and harnessed wind and sun—
energies to keep us as warm as your womb.
You have molded mountains and mesas, gulfs and seaboards,
plains and deltas, and rivers and lakes—like play yards
to secure us and provide room to romp and run.
Furry and feathery, silky and prickly animals are woven
into our lives like friends that you knew we would need and love.
Oh, Earth, You are a good Mother, lavish and loyal.

—DONNA WAHLERT

GOLDEN ROADS

I no longer set the alarm on the clock. Long before it is my wont to wake up, a mockingbird alerts me to the day with acoustical acrobatics.

As the sun's rays touch the tips of an army of cypresses, then bend down to caress the pink filaments of the mimosa, and dance their way down and come to rest on a green carpet of grass, I think about the many ways by which nature brings meaning and richness to our lives.

The pyramids are a sight to behold, and who can forget a trek in the foothills of the Himalayas or a boat ride on the Danube, but there is pure magic in watching a dove build its nest in the branches of a palmetto.

So, welcome to the pyramid of the rose, the Danube of the wisteria, the towering peak of the ocotillo.

Welcome, also, to the Taj Mahal of the peacock, the royal barge of the grackle, and the temple of the caparisoned elephant.

At the crepuscular hour, a low-flying owl startled me out of my reverie in the backyard.

A full moon smiled upon this incident.

Said the moon: "An owl is an ordinary creature until you look at it extraordinarily."

So are a blade of grass, a raindrop on a broad lotus leaf, and a scent of jasmine made special to embrace the circumference of the earth.

All roads are golden, for the gold is in our eyes.

—RAMNATH SUBRAMANIAN

EARTH BLESSING

May the sun bless you
with laughter and fire
and the moon glow iridescence
upon your night journeys

May the rains of dawn refresh
each day, and trees
grow lush for shady retreat

May flowers rise
to lead your dance;
the wind chant your song

May birds feather your heart
to soften sorrow,
and the Earth clothed in green
velvet feed you eternity

May the words and deeds
of your life
be the mingling bands
of the rainbow

—SUE HOLLOWAY

THE EARTH SINGS

The Earth sings—
Dance to the beat.

—JUNE COTNER

The miracle is to walk on the green earth in the present moment, to appreciate the peace and beauty that are available now.

—THICH NHAT HANH

If we look at the path, we do not see the sky. We are earth people on a spiritual journey to the stars. Our quest, our earth walk, is to look within, to know who we are, to see that we are connected to all things, that there is no separation, only in the mind.

—AUTHOR UNKNOWN

May our walking on the earth
be as gentle as the union
of the butterfly and the flower.

—TRADITIONAL BUDDHIST BLESSING

Observe the marvels as they happen around you. Don't claim them. Feel the beauty moving through and be silent.

—RUMI

Touch the earth, love the earth, honor the earth, her plains, her valleys, her hills, and her seas: rest your spirit in her solitary places.

—HENRY BESTON

Be humble for you are made of Earth. Be noble for you are made of stars.

—SERBIAN PROVERB

And forget not that the earth delights
to feel your bare feet and the winds long
to play with your hair.

—KHALIL GIBRAN

I BELIEVE

I don't believe in magic. I believe in the sun and the stars, the water, the tides, the floods, the owls, the hawks flying, the river running, the wind talking. They're measurements. They tell us how healthy things are. How healthy we are. Because we and they are the same. That's what I believe in.

—BILLY FRANK, JR., NISQUALLY TRIBE

Author Index

Permissions and Acknowledgments

Grateful acknowledgment is made to the authors and publishers for the use of the following material. Every effort has been made to contact original sources. If notified, the publishers will be pleased to rectify an omission in future editions.

Lisa Poje Angelos for "A Prayer for Wisdom."

Antler for "What the God Says through Me."

Joan Marie Arbogast for "A Proverb." www.joanmariearbogast.com

Ellen Bass for "When You Return" from *Like a Beggar*. Copyright © 2014 by Ellen Bass. Reprinted with the permission of The Permissions Company, Inc. on behalf of Copper Canyon Press, www.coppercanyonpress.org, www.ellenbass.com

Mike W. Blottenberger for "The Place No One Knew."

Gayle Brandeis for "Deer at Santa Sabina" and "Fig Grove." www.gaylebrandeis.com

Cindy Breedlove for "One Summer Night."

Stones Music. All rights reserved. Used by permission.
www.roughstonesmusic.com

Barbara Crooker for "Building a Compost Pile," "Listen," "Listen," "Praise Song," and "Walking Alone on a Thickly Starred Night." "Listen" on p. 127 is excerpted from *Line Dance*. Copyright © 2008 by Barbara Crooker, published by WordTech Communications; "Praise Song" is excerpted from *Radiance: Poems*. Copyright © 2005 by Barbara Crooker, published by WordTech Communications. Permission granted by Barbara Crooker. www.barbaracrooker.com

Corrine De Winter for "After the Long Gathering," "Earth Speaks," and "Remember." www.corrinedewinter.com

Magie Dominic for "The Path." www.magiedominic.blogspot.com

Annie Dougherty for "The Inn in the Cedars."

Susan J. Erickson for "Spirit Ear" and "The Third Beatitude."

Janice A. Farringer for "Simplicity." www.amidlifebooksandpoetry.com

Sheila Forsyth for "Working Together."

Charles Ghigna for "One" www.fathergoose.com

Michael S. Glaser for "A Concept of Grace" and "Tugging Us toward Wonder." www.michaelsglaser.com

Terri Glass for "Just Another Day." www.terriglass.com

Ingrid Goff-Maidoff for "Golden Pearl." www.tendingjoy.com

Taylor Graham for "Earth Day" and "Giving Back." www.somersetsunset.net

Theresa Mary Grass for "Earth Song" and "O Creator."

Annette Gulati for "The Earth's Dance." www.annettegulati.com

Maryanne Hannan for "Doxology," "Go Ahead," and "Says Mother Earth." www.mhannan.com

selections granted by Mata Amritanandamayi Center and Janine Canan. www.amma.org, www.janinecanan.com

Barb Mayer for "Think for Today" and "When We Live in Harmony with Nature." www.barbmayer.com

Gary E. McCormick for "Thank You, Thank You."

Nancy H. McCray for "Unto the Hills" by Bob McCray.

Maureen McQuerry for "October Dusk."

Karen Minnich-Sadler for "To Care for the Earth."

Felicia Mitchell for "Bear Calls" excerpted from *Waltzing with Horses*. Copyright © 2014 by Felicia Mitchell, published by Press 53. Permission granted by Felicia Mitchell. www.feliciamitchell.net

Sudie Nostrand for "Eagles."

Cheryl Paulson for "A Barefoot Blessing" and "For the Children." www.breathingroomcenter.com

Nita Penfold for "Oh Great Planet of Our Birth." www.nitapenfold.com

Mary Lenore Quigley for "Season of Surprises." www.q2ink.com

Zoraida Rivera Morales for "Come to Meet."

Kenneth Salzmann for "Theology."

Hilda Lachney Sanderson for "Wild Geese."

Judith Sornberger for "Also, There Are the Kindnesses of Birds."

Cassie Premo Steele for "In Between" and "What I Want to Tell You About the Rain." The latter poem is excerpted from *The Pomegranate Papers*. Copyright © 2012 by Cassie Premo Steele, published by Unbound Content. Permission granted by Cassie Premo Steele. www.cassiepremosteele.com, www.earthjoywriting.com

Ramnath Subramanian for "Golden Roads" and "A Toast to Morning."

Christine Swanberg for "Hummingbird Whisperer."

Patti Tana for "The Secret of Life" excerpted from *Any Given Day*. Copyright © 2011 by Patti Tana, published by Whittier Publications. Permission granted by Patti Tana. www.pattitana.com

Arlene Tribbia for "An Afternoon Spent Watching Flights." http://arlenetribbia.com/wp

Donna Wahlert for "I Care So Much About the Earth," Lovely Earth," "To Earth," and "Wintering."

Joanna M. Weston for "The Cadence of the Earth."

About the Author

June Cotner is the author or editor of thirty-four books, including the bestselling *Graces, Bedside Prayers,* and *House Blessings.* Her books altogether have sold more than one million copies and have been featured in many national publications including *USA Today, Better Homes and Gardens, Woman's Day,* and *Family Circle.* June has appeared on national television and radio programs.

June's latest love and avocation is giving presentations on adopting prisoner-trained shelter dogs. In 2011, she adopted Indy, a chocolate Lab/Doberman mix (a LabraDobie!), from the Freedom Tails program at Stafford Creek Corrections Center in Aberdeen, Washington. June works with Indy daily to build on the wonderful obedience skills he mastered in the program. She and Indy have appeared on the television shows *AM Northwest* (Portland, OR) and *New Day Northwest* (Seattle).

A graduate of the University of California at Berkeley, June is the mother of two grown children and lives in Poulsbo, Washington with her husband. Her hobbies include yoga, hiking, and playing with her two grandchildren.

For more information, please visit June's website at
www.junecotner.com.

Author photograph by Barb Mayer Photography.